prayer
encounters

Changing the World One Prayer at a Time

Paul M. Burns

WestBow
P R E S S
A DIVISION OF THOMAS NELSON

WestBow Press books may be ordered through booksellers or by contacting:

WestBow Press
A Division of Thomas Nelson
1663 Liberty Drive
Bloomington, IN 47403
www.westbowpress.com
1-(866) 928-1240

ISBN: 978-1-4497-5194-4 (sc)
ISBN: 978-1-4497-5195-1 (e)

Library of Congress Control Number: 2012908860

Printed in the United States of America

WestBow Press rev. date: 06/01/2012

table of contents

acknowledgments

I would like to acknowledge the many people who played a critical role in the creation of this book.

Thanks to my parents, who have been praying with me and for me my whole life. They taught me that prayer is essential to a life of faith and that it really matters.

Thanks to my wife, Jennifer, for her constant support and love.

Further thanks to those who read my early attempts at this project: Michael Brundeen, Mark Bryan, Sara Bowling, Crystal Caviness, and my dad. They each significantly shaped this book and helped me to see its potential and value.

Very special thanks to my editor, Elizabeth Lindsey. She helped me turn a well-intentioned attempt at written communication into a book.

I would also like to thank all the people who allowed me to share their stories. Although most of their names have been changed in this book, they will be forever written on my heart.

And finally, I would like to thank Jesus Christ, who encounters me daily and pushes me toward encountering others in his name.

Paul Burns

introduction

While serving as a chaplain at an inner-city hospital in Dallas, Texas, I was required to make contact with as many patients as possible. The areas with which I was charged were the neonatal intensive care unit (NICU) and the antepartum and postpartum units—the maternity areas, for better or for worse. Too often for worse.

As a pastor still very much in training, I had not yet stopped feeling a bit trepidatious about walking into the room of a total stranger whose religious beliefs I did not know. This was quite different from the cold calls I used to make as a financial advisor. I remember those first few timid knocks accompanied by, "H . . . hello? Chaplain here. Can I come in?" I did not know what to expect. Would they call security or what? Imagine knocking on some stranger's bedroom door, "Chaplain here, coming in."

But whether it was a joyful mother with child and family or a bereft and lonely woman suffering the unimaginable, I was always welcomed in. Happy families always accepted a blessing for the new baby. Grieving families never turned down a listening ear and a prayer of comfort. In fact, during the whole summer I spent at the hospital, visiting twenty to thirty patients a day, I was never turned down for prayer.

Something about being in a hospital opens a person up to prayer.

I remember my first encounter with a husband and wife who had lost a child. The administrative assistant of pastoral care handed me a short note: "Fetal demise. Spanish only. Room 723." I had spent one week in training, shadowing an experienced mentor. Why was she not handling this one? She was out for the week.

I called a translator, and she met me outside the patient's room. I briefly described the scenario. We both gulped and took a deep breath. She knew her role: translate, although most of what had happened needed no translation. Did I understand my role, a man standing between God and a couple in deep mourning? I felt greatly inadequate.

We entered. I kind of pushed the translator in front of me. After all, some explanation of why I was there was needed. Not a doctor, not a nurse, but a chaplain. They send doctors to patients who can be fixed. They send chaplains in for the rest. Chaplains say, "I'm sorry."

I will never forget the eyes of the helpless husband—big, scared eyes. His wife's face was ashen with grief, her eyes cast downward. He explained to me that this was their third lost child. He was afraid that this was too much for his wife.

The translator's job was no easier. She had to repeat a difficult story of infant death. Possibly one she had heard before or even experienced herself.

It quickly became clear that no words of consolation or advice would be even remotely helpful or appropriate. What could I possibly tell this couple about how to cope and move on from this?

I offered the only thing I had, prayer. The husband's eyes lit up as if to say, "Yes! That's what we need! Please!" We all joined hands, including the translator, as I lifted up the couple's pain to the Lord. The woman was in tears. Her first tears. She began to talk now and make eye contact. The healing had begun.

It was as if the prayer had turned on a light.

As I was leaving, the husband walked after me and, in broken English, thanked me and asked if I would come back to pray with them the next day.

I had always known on some level that prayer is important, but on that day I learned how much people really need it. It was not that the couple needed my words or my presence. It was God's presence they had so desperately needed. At times in our lives, God seems so absent or so far away that we need a person in the flesh to represent his presence. We need a prayer encounter.

As I shoved off into the "regular world" of church ministry, I assumed it would be different. I assumed I would meet a world of resistance—but instead I met a whole world of need.

As the pastor of a small Presbyterian church in Nashville, Tennessee, I have yet to find a person in need who refuses prayer. Church members wanting prayer, sure, that is to be expected. But I have also prayed with strangers in parking lots, grocery stores, doctors' offices, coffee shops, basketball courts, restaurants—you name it. Everyone seems to need and want prayer.

Something about life opens a person up to prayer.

Sooner or later we all run into something we have no control over: some situation, illness, bad weather, job loss, rejection, addiction, some pain that makes us full of need for God and each other. Realizing this puts us in the perfect position for prayer.

God can sometimes feel so distant, if not nonexistent. This is when we need people who will represent God for us and bring us before him in prayer. We need someone who will take a chance and knock on our door, not with a sales pitch but with something real—with the grace of God

Prayer is the answer. Prayer connects us with God and with each other. In prayer we are encountered by a real God, one who is more powerful than the powers that bind us. One who has even walked in our shoes. One who comes to us when we are helpless. One who accepts us when no one else does. One who sees through our shame to the hurt that is underneath. One who forgives and heals and makes us useful to him and the world he created.

In this book I share some of the prayer encounters I have experienced and witnessed over the last few years. These encounters have changed my life over and over again. They have connected me to people I will never forget and to a God who will never forget me.

Throughout this book I invite you to begin a journey of praying with others. Each chapter includes scripture, a prayer encounter story, a reflection, questions to consider, a prayer challenge, and a prayer to pray. Whether you read this book by yourself or with a group, I hope you will take the challenge of praying with others. Unless otherwise noted, all scripture comes from the English Standard Version.

If you are leading a group through this book, consider starting each session by inviting members to share any prayer encounters they have experienced as a result of taking the prayer challenge from the previous session. I hope you will also share your stories with me at www.prayerencounters.com. I would love to hear them!

Whether you are a church person or not, God can use you to bring life to others. A minute of your time can change life forever, even for a total stranger, and it can be done with grace and ease. In doing so, you can both fulfill your duty as a disciple of Christ and, at the same time, receive the life you yourself hunger for.

Will you pray with me?

O God of grace and power, I need you more than I can even express. I ask you to lift up this hurting world into your heart. Love it, forgive it, heal it, and give it life. Use me to stand with others in encountering you in prayer. Give me the courage to knock on the doors I encounter in my daily life, knowing that great needs await to be met. In the graceful name of Jesus I pray. Amen.

1

and a little child shall lead them

Thomas said to him, "Lord, we do not know where you are going. How can we know the way?" Jesus said to him, "I am the way, and the truth, and the life. No one comes to the Father except through me. If you had known me, you would have known my Father also. From now on you do know him and have seen him." John 14:5-7

PRAYER ENCOUNTER

Over the last three years, the church I serve has hosted a summer basketball program. Through it we have gotten to know our neighborhood in amazing ways. We have received new life through this ministry.

During this time, we have encountered over a hundred youth who live within walking distance of our church building. Many of our members used to see these girls and boys with their loud voices, uncontrolled energy, and baggy clothing and fear that gangs were taking over our neighborhood. Now they see faces they know and are learning to love. The neighborhood's children are becoming our children.

One summer, the youngest but feistiest of the players, all of ten years of age and four feet eleven in height, came to me and said, "I want to be baptized."

I am not sure where he even got the idea. I do not remember talking about it with any of the kids. For the most part, we just play basketball. I asked him why he wanted to be baptized.

"I want to be clean," he told me, as if he had been a lifelong criminal. "And I want my mom to be clean, too. I don't want to do it until my mom does it with me, though, and I don't know if that can happen." He stared at the floor.

"What do you mean?" I asked, still amazed we were even having this conversation.

"She does some really bad things, and the neighborhood all knows about it. They all call my house 'the crack house.' She does bad stuff with men." He seemed utterly defeated. He looked up at me, eyes full of hurt, and asked, "Could you talk to her?"

Honestly, her problems seemed way out of my league. I am good for some food and a gas card and the occasional electric bill, but this—drugs and prostitution—was serious stuff. How could problems like these be right in our neighborhood?

After a few weeks of not really knowing what I could do to help, I decided to walk over and meet the boy's mother. She was eight months pregnant. No husband. I told her that her son wanted to be baptized. She began to weep.

"I know. It's amazing! I don't know how it happened. He's always been special." Tears streamed down her cheeks.

"Why are you crying?" I could not discern whether these were tears of joy or distress.

"Because I won't be able to see it happen."

"Why not?" My bewilderment increased.

"Everybody knows about me. I couldn't show up at the church. I'm so ashamed!" Her sobbing intensified. "I feel trapped, and I don't know how to get out of this life."

What could I say? I whispered a quiet prayer, "Lord, help me." Then the words came to my lips, "I can't help you, but Christ can. I don't know how, but he will show you the way out."

She looked at me with despair in her eyes.

"Will you let me pray with you?" I asked.

She nodded. We prayed for Christ to show her a way out and to give her a new life.

A few weeks later, she had the baby, a little girl. The state took the baby because of the drugs in her system. A few days later, the mother, in her state of addiction, desperation, and depression, had a night that landed her in jail.

The Sunday she was released, she walked into our evening praise service, eyes cried out, and said wearily but with resolve, "The night after I got put in jail, I realized I couldn't do this on my own. I'm tired. I'm tired of fighting. I asked Jesus to change me, and I can't explain it, but something happened. I want to be baptized, but not until my baby can be baptized with me. I need help. I need my baby."

Several of us in the service gathered around her, and we prayed.

Three weeks later I baptized the son, the mother, and the baby. I cannot tell you how it all happened, but it happened. All I did was pray.

She then entered a rehab program, where the tough but clear road to wellness began. Her struggles are not over, but she and her two children are healthy and safe, and a new life for all of them has begun.

REFLECTION

I recently had a conversation with a fellow Presbyterian that began, "You know what I really don't like? Evangelism! What do you think about evangelism?"

As a pastor, this is the kind of conversation I generally dread. It usually starts with an extreme opinion like "The choir really stinks. What do you think?" or "I think the president is a schmuck. What do you think?"

It is a losing proposition. You either have to agree, which leads to that person telling the choir that Pastor Paul says they stink, or you end up in an unpleasant debate you can never win.

My response was to tell him the story you have just read. Evangelism is not a proposition. It is not a strategy. It is not convincing people they are wrong and you are right. It is a story of Good News that you and I can find ourselves caught up in if we follow the trail of Christ.

The Good News is that there is a way out of the old life and a way into a new life. We are not stuck.

Only Christ could save a family through the faith and desire of a fifth-grade boy.

I remember this story every time someone tells me about feeling stuck. I know the Way out! I have encountered him. I have seen him in action.

Prayer is the key. You can tell someone about Christ. You can tell someone how a relationship with Christ has changed your life and can change the lives of others. But it is in prayer that we can truly bring another into an encounter with Christ. He works through people of faith, but he is the only one who can give a person a new life.

QUESTIONS TO CONSIDER

1. Can you think of a time in your life when you felt stuck? What did you do?
2. Do you know someone who is currently stuck? Perhaps that person's problem seems too large for you to get involved with. But what could you do to help?
3. Have you ever prayed with another person? How do you feel about praying with other people?

PRAYER CHALLENGE

If you know someone who feels stuck, pray for that person. Or better yet, offer to pray with that person. Ask Christ for guidance out of the situation.

PRAYER

O Lord, I do not have all the answers or solutions to the problems of life. Show me your way. Give me the courage to get involved with people who are in need, even if I do not know how to help. In the name of Christ I pray. Amen.

2

parker's prayer

For you did not receive the spirit of slavery to fall back into fear,
but you have received the Spirit of adoption as sons, by whom
we cry, "Abba! Father!" Romans 8:15

PRAYER ENCOUNTER

Parker is, without a doubt, the most popular boy amongst the
neighborhood basketball crowd. When he walks into the gym at our
church, everyone's attention shifts to him. He is hard not to notice.
He is six foot seven and nothing but muscle and tattoos.

He has played with us for each of the three years we have had
our Summer Hoops program. In that period, he has gone from high
school basketball star to scholarship athlete at Western Kentucky
University to doing nothing.

I do not know exactly how he lost his scholarship, but I know
he was disappointed and perhaps ashamed. Right now he works at
IHOP and hopes to become a fireman.

I must admit that when Parker first started playing with us, I was
quite intimidated. He would come in with his entourage of equally
formidable young men. Nobody messed with them, especially not
the pastor (me).

Week after week I led a halftime devotion, never knowing if anyone was paying attention. Parker and company often disappeared when I began to speak. This last summer was different, though.

When Parker first arrived at the gym last summer, I was shocked and touched when he greeted me with a hug. "Hey, Pastor Paul. Good to see you." This became his weekly greeting. When I would call to everyone for the devotion, it was Parker who gathered them up. He paid particular attention to the younger boys. If they were getting picked on, he was right there to stop it. He could stop it with a look.

After we play, we have dinner together. Before we line up at the kitchen counter to fill our plates, we pray. We hold hands and bow our heads, and I thank God for the food and also for their lives, their families, and their futures.

One week I had gathered us together and started to pray when Parker spoke up, "I got this one, Pastor Paul." Taken aback, I stepped aside.

Usually when I pray, I have to pepper the prayer with half a dozen "Quiet please!"s, but not when Parker prayed. The gym and the thirty-five young men and women in it were silent and deferential.

His prayer was strong and full of thanks and respect. I do not remember much of what he said, but I do remember how he began: "Father God . . ."

As his words rang out, I remembered that Parker does not know his father. At that moment, Parker changed before my eyes from a street-tough player to a boy without a dad.

I understood his hug.

REFLECTION

While in seminary, I served as an intern at a church in downtown Austin, Texas. I led an adult Sunday school class that studied the sermon text for the week. The class was filled with highly educated, thoughtful, and caring men and women.

One week we were studying John 17 in which Jesus prays to his Father in heaven on behalf of his disciples. The word *Father* is used over and over again, showing the intimacy of the Son and the Father. Naturally when I closed in prayer, I began, "O heavenly Father . . ."

A woman in the class approached me afterward with anger on her face and demanded, "What are they teaching you at that seminary? Aren't they teaching you to use inclusive language to describe God? I am highly offended that you used the word *Father* in that prayer."

I explained that we were taught to draw on the great diversity of biblical language used for God, which includes *Father*. I asked her why she was offended, and she responded that there are many people for whom *father* is not a good word. They have suffered abuse, neglect, and the absence of their fathers. She admitted that she had not experienced this because she had a good relationship with her father, but she knew others who did not.

We all have wounds. If we never address them, they will fester and consume us. If *father* means pain, fear, or absence, maybe, instead of dismissing *father* from our language and our lives, we might seek a new model.

I do not pretend to know what it is like to not have a good earthly father because I have been greatly blessed by mine. But I do know what it is like to be enslaved by a spirit of fear, as Paul wrote of to the Romans (8:15). It keeps a person from healing, forgiveness, and new relationships for fear of rejection and further pain. It keeps us isolated and makes us cold and bitter.

I do not believe we ever outgrow our need for a parent. To call God "Abba, Father" in prayer is to recognize that we are his children and he loves and accepts each of us.

Perhaps the world has left you orphaned. I know a family that will be glad to adopt you: Father, Son, and Holy Spirit. It is a big family but one that always has room for one more.

Questions to Consider

1. What do you picture when you think of God? Do you see something or someone?
2. Can you think of anyone in your life who has been a father or a mother to you who is not your biological parent?
3. Do you know someone who is in need of a mother or a father?

Prayer Challenge

Pray with a youth this week and, if possible, one who does not know one or both parents.

Prayer

Dear heavenly Father, Mother of us all, thank you for the parents you have given to me in whatever form. Help me to be a parent to a child, youth, or adult who needs one. Just as Jesus prayed for those whom you entrusted to him, help me to pray for the ones you have entrusted to me. In the name of our older brother Jesus, I pray. Amen.

3

"how do i get the holy spirit inside of me?"

I will sprinkle clean water on you, and you shall be clean from all your uncleannesses, and from all your idols I will cleanse you. And I will give you a new heart, and a new spirit I will put within you. And I will remove the heart of stone from your flesh and give you a heart of flesh. And I will put my Spirit within you, and cause you to walk in my statutes and be careful to obey my rules. Ezekiel 36:25-27

PRAYER ENCOUNTER

Our Summer Hoops basketball program meets a need in a neighborhood filled with youth who have nothing to do. There really is not anything within walking distance of their homes besides a little grocery store and a few churches. No community center.

I had a conversation with a man who works for the YMCA about what it would take to get a Y in our neighborhood. He said, "Form a board, raise the money, build the building, and then let us know. We will consider putting our name on it." It was not the answer I was looking for.

He went on to say, "Paul, consider something. You've got a gym at your church. Kids play basketball there. Your neighborhood already has a community center. Your church. Just go with that. Make it happen."

The first summer we opened up the gym to the neighborhood, we had over eighty kids, as young as ten and all the way up to nineteen, play with us. Now it is such a part of who we are as a church, we are not even sure we want the YMCA or a municipal recreation center to move into our neighborhood. We love these kids.

On a blazing hot day near the close of that first summer, one of the high-school boys, Ronnie, shyly came up to me and said, "I wanna get baptized." I was surprised. It was the first thing he had ever really said to me, and we had had no altar call or anything that afternoon. Just basketball and a brief devotion. I told him I wanted to talk with him more about it. Another boy, Jermal, was standing nearby, and he said, "Can I come and listen?" This was becoming an epidemic!

I asked Ronnie why he wanted to be baptized, and he told me he wanted to change the way he lived his life. I asked him if he trusted in Jesus as his savior. He did. I explained that it is ultimately the Holy Spirit working inside of us who changes us and that baptism is a sign of that new life.

Jermal was listening carefully. He raised his hand. "Pastor Paul, I've been baptized already, but I still do bad stuff. How can I get the Holy Spirit inside of me?"

When he said this, I wanted to hit the pause button and both cry for the boy and praise God for putting this question in his heart. I replied, "You just need to ask God to forgive you and fill you with the Holy Spirit."

He looked at me thoughtfully but clearly puzzled. "How do I do that?"

"Pray."

He took my hand and Ronnie's, and he prayed the most sincere prayer of repentance I have ever heard. A seventh-grade boy! He begged God to forgive him and then to fill him with the Holy Spirit.

Ronnie was baptized the next month. Soon after, Jermal and his brother, Wallace, made a public profession of faith and joined the church.

I do not see Jermal very often. When he does show up, I always tell him the same thing. He smiles because he knows what I am going to say: "Don't forget, you've got the Holy Spirit inside you now."

I hope he remembers it every day. I hope he remembers it when he is faced with the tough choices that boys in our neighborhood encounter every day. To do drugs or not. To fight or not. To rob or not. To join a gang or not. To hate or to love.

I like our church being a community center that attracts the neighborhood's children. It opens us up to the Holy Spirit as well. We get a fresh whiff of the Spirit every time we open the door and welcome others into our lives. The stale air of comfort and complacency is swept out, and something new is made again.

REFLECTION

Most houses used to have a parlor, later called a living room. It was kept spic and span and had all the nice stuff in it. The living room was not for playing in. It was for company, the kind of company that just likes to talk and drink coffee. As a kid, this seemed like the worst way I could possibly imagine spending my time. No fun at all!

When I was a boy, we had both a living room and a den. The den was where we were most at home. It was where we were a family. We played games and watched TV together in our den. We rarely used our living room. That room remained a place where kids could get in trouble if they made a mess or did not use proper manners.

The days of formal living rooms are fast fading away, but the concept remains very much alive in churches all over the place. Churches still have spaces where children and youth are not very welcome. They might break something or be noisy.

A man in our church told me he once complained to a pastor that some kids were disturbing the church service, and he asked the pastor if he would do something about it. The pastor responded, "That disturbance is the sound of life. Without it, we are dead."

Whether you are a church person or not, children keep us open to new life. They keep us from becoming set in our ways. Relating to children requires us to learn and to try new things. You cannot have an intelligent conversation with teenagers today without knowing something about the things that matter to them. Children of all ages remind us of simple joys and basic needs. In them we see who we once were and could be again.

We need children at all costs. The day you or I have no room for children is the day our hearts have become hard and closed off.

QUESTIONS TO CONSIDER

1. When was the last time you had a child in your home?
2. What new things have you tried in the last year?
3. What do you remember about church and church people when you were a child?

PRAYER CHALLENGE

Pick a child in your neighborhood to pray for regularly.

PRAYER

Lord, help me to be open to children in my life. Show me a child you would like me to pray for. Restore to me the heart of a child—open, excited, and receptive to your Holy Spirit. In the name of Christ, who was once a child, I pray. Amen.

---- **4** ----

six-year-old jesus

I have been crucified with Christ. It is no longer I who live, but Christ who lives in me. And the life I now live in the flesh I live by faith in the Son of God, who loved me and gave himself for me. Galatians 2:20

PRAYER ENCOUNTER

One of the missions of our church is delivering Christmas and Easter food boxes to struggling families. We get names from local school counselors, who are often the most aware of the needs of families in our city.

We load up on a Saturday and go two by two with a list of names and addresses, and cars full of boxes laden with ham or turkey, fixin's, and love.

When we deliver the food, we talk to the families and ask about their lives. Then we offer prayer and a blessing. Everyone comes back with lots of smiles and stories.

The week before Easter a few years ago, my delivery partner, Sajeev, and I knocked on the door of a very nice-looking house. We wondered if perhaps we had the wrong address. A little boy opened up the door with a big smile. His mother let us in and showed us to the kitchen. I was not sure there was any food in it. The boy grabbed some of the candy from the food box and ran off to his room.

The mother told us this was not her house. It belonged to her sister, who was out of town. They had just moved here from Chattanooga, Tennessee, where she had been in a women's shelter. Her son's father had died, and she was trying to get into a housing program here in Nashville. She said she had begun the day praying for food because they were out and she did not know how she would get more. When she got our call, she knew God had answered her.

The boy came back with a broken iPod and a half-used bottle of cologne. He gave Sajeev the iPod and me the cologne. "For you!" How could we say no?

I invited us to hold hands and pray. There we stood, a human family, heads bowed. I prayed for all the needs mentioned by the mother and gave thanks for the generosity of her son.

I had started to say Amen, when the mother dropped to her knees—and when I say dropped, I mean she literally dropped, hard—still holding our hands. She lifted up her head and cried out to the Lord in a prayer that stunned me with its sincerity and emotion. She gave thanks and asked God's blessing on us and on our church.

We left her with the box of food, and we took away hearts full of blessing. Sajeev asked me, "Why do you think a six-year-old boy would have a half-used bottle of cologne in his room?" It hit me like a ten-pound ham—it had belonged to his father. The boy had given me his most precious possession.

Giving what is most precious for the sake of another is at the heart of the Good News of Christ.

Jesus was once a six-year-old boy, and that day he was again.

REFLECTION

My natural inclination when this boy brought out his gifts was to politely decline them. After all, Sajeev and I were the ones who were doing the giving that day. The boy and his mother were just supposed to receive our charity and give thanks for it, right?

Yet, to refuse the boy's gifts would have been to shut down the possibility of having any kind of relationship with him. When we do not accept the gifts they offer us, we keep people at a distance. We do not allow ourselves to enjoy their blessings, and we deny them the gift of giving those blessings to us. We deny that they have something valuable to give.

It also did not occur to me that the boy's mother might want to share in the prayer with us instead of standing by passively while Sajeev and I prayed for her and her son. What I had forgotten was that, like receiving gifts, praying together builds relationships with others. Walls are broken down, distances bridged, differences dissolved.

In the gospels, Jesus was always building relationships with those around him. He did not just parachute into the world, die for our sins, and helicopter out again. He connected with people. He lived in relationship with others.

Jesus gave, and he also received.

One of my favorite stories is found in Luke 7:36-50. Jesus was dining at the house of a Pharisee when "a woman of the city, who was a sinner" interrupted their meal. She brought an alabaster flask of oil with which to anoint Jesus' feet, but first she anointed them with her tears. She wiped her tears off with her hair, then kissed his feet, and then anointed his feet with the oil. The Pharisee was outraged that Jesus would allow this woman to touch him. Jesus' response to the woman was to offer her forgiveness. He knew what she truly needed, and he gave it to her.

Jesus built relationships with whoever was receptive to him, regardless of what anyone, even the Pharisees, thought. This woman gave him what she had to give, and he gave her what he had to give.

For a lasting relationship, we must both give and receive. If we do only the giving, it will not work. If we do only the receiving, it will not work. To not receive as well as to give would be like only breathing out or only breathing in. Both actions are necessary for us to live.

Praying together opens us up to Christ and to each other. Through our prayer, the Spirit connects us to Christ, and Christ connects us to one another. He blesses all parties with two amazing gifts: himself and each other.

QUESTIONS TO CONSIDER

1. In what ways do you help other people?
2. In what ways do you allow other people to help you?
3. Do you find it hard to receive gifts or help or friendship from other people? Why or why not?

PRAYER CHALLENGE

The next time you pray with someone, share your prayer needs with that person and give that person an opportunity to pray for you.

PRAYER

O great giving God, thank you for the life you have given to me. Help me to receive all that you desire to give to me. Give me the courage to share both my gifts and my needs with others. In the name of the one who gave his life for me, I pray. Amen.

5

christmas ham

*Therefore I tell you, do not be anxious about your life, what you
will eat or what you will drink, nor about your body, what you
will put on. Is not life more than food, and the body more than
clothing?* Matthew 6:25

PRAYER ENCOUNTER

The main hub for our church's neighborhood is a family-owned
grocery store called Compton's. Over the years, Compton's has
become a partner for us in our food ministries. When Nashville
was flooded in 2010, the store set up a giant box in its entrance to
receive food, household goods, and personal items for our church to
distribute to flood victims.

Through this I got to know the manager, Dolly. When we came
to pick up the donations, Dolly pulled out money from her own
purse to help. She called out to the rest of the employees to chip in,
too. I collected over one hundred dollars in a heartbeat.

The next December, we ordered hams for our Christmas food
box delivery mission through Compton's at cost. When I came to
pick up the one hundred hams, there was a lot of excitement at the
store. They had never had anybody buy meat in that quantity before.
Together we all felt like Santa Claus!

Now, I love ham. Just the idea of driving around with a thousand pounds of ham in my SUV is like Christmas morning, and it had me smiling.

As I was paying the bill, though, I noticed Dolly in the manager's booth. She was not smiling. She was crying as she was trying to go through invoices. She was eight months pregnant.

After I had paid, I walked over to the booth and asked her what was going on. She told me that her blood pressure was really high and she was probably going to have to be on bed rest for the rest of her pregnancy. She was so worried about the baby, she just could not focus on her work.

I asked if I could pray with her. She nodded her head vigorously and tearfully. We both kind of leaned in so as to not be too obvious. After all, this was her workplace and she was the boss. I did not want to embarrass her in any way. She took my hand, and we bowed our heads. I prayed for health, peace, and faith for her and for good and timely delivery of the baby. After the prayer, she took a deep breath and asked, "It's going to be okay, isn't it?" Her voiced quavered. "Yes," I said.

A couple of months passed, and when I entered the store to pick up something for dinner, there was Dolly awaiting me with a huge smile and a huge hug. The delivery had gone great, and she and the baby were both healthy.

Some things in life are even better than ham.

REFLECTION

One of the biggest shifts in our society has been the move from an agrarian to an industrial economy and culture. The impact becomes greater with each year of human existence.

In an agrarian community, people depended upon each other for many things. Some families produced corn, some wheat. Some poultry, some cattle. Some made furniture. Some sold household goods. There may have been only one doctor, and he did everything. There may have been only one preacher, one teacher, one dentist.

If you needed something, you depended upon another person to provide it.

Now, of course, you do not need to even leave your house for anything, really. We rely upon corporations, machines, and delivery trucks to meet our material needs. In the process, we interact with fewer people.

I grew up watching the TV series *Little House on the Prairie*. If I ever complained about anything, my dad's stock response was, "On *Little House on the Prairie*, they didn't have TV, cars, [fill in the blank]. They walked, entertained themselves, and took nothing for granted like you do."

Okay, maybe I am exaggerating a bit, but it made an impact on me. Even now I try to look at our world today through Pa Ingalls's eyes. How would he see this world? I imagine he would be most shocked by the disintegration of human community. Most of us live within walking distance of hundreds of people, but how many of them have we even met, let alone gotten to know?

We are not forced to know people. We do not need them in a material sense. But our souls need human connection. Through the virtual world of the Internet, we desperately seek each other all over the globe, yet we ignore our next-door neighbor.

I am guilty of this. I want to be able to turn my human relationships on or off at my convenience, just like my computer. Most days I just keep my eyes down and move forward, accomplishing my tasks and fulfilling my personal desires. Meanwhile, people are in need of human connection all around me.

When we pray with one another, a new community begins to form, one called the Kingdom of God.

Questions to Consider

1. Can you name your ten closest neighbors? Five? Two? One?
2. What are the places you go to regularly where other people are?
3. Have you ever seen someone who looked troubled, but you did not say or do anything about it? Why not?

PRAYER CHALLENGE

During this next week, keep your eye out for someone who seems to be having a bad day. Ask that person to share what is going on. Offer to pray with that person. I realize this is a daunting challenge, but give it a shot. What is the worst thing that could happen? Low risk, high reward.

PRAYER

Lord, give me the courage to connect with others. Bring to my attention this coming week a person who needs an encouraging word and a prayer. In the name of the great human connector, Christ, I pray. Amen.

6

---

wrestling with poverty

If one member suffers, all suffer together. 1 Corinthians 12:26

PRAYER ENCOUNTER

One of the annual missions of our church is called Project JOY (Joyous Offering of Youth). It is an Appalachian ministry. Every fall, with the help of twenty-four other Middle Tennessee churches and dozens of people who live in our neighborhood, we gather warm clothing, school supplies, food, children's books, and Bibles and travel to Harlan, Kentucky. The National Guard allows us to set up in its armory there.

Harlan is a coal-mining town whose heyday was some fifty years ago. Many families live up in the hills and have very little of anything. Children often go without. Winter is harsh.

The poverty cycle in Harlan is extreme. We realize that one day a year will not break it. Our desire is to provide some needed goods, some hope, and some joy.

A few years ago, we decided to put up a prayer station near the armory's exit. I set up two folding chairs, one for me and one for another person. I taped a sign with the words "Need Prayer?" on the back of the empty chair.

Most of the folks are too focused on getting what they need for themselves and their children to think about prayer, but each year I get about a dozen people who will sit down for it.

I have listened to one heartbreak story after another. I have seen many tears shed and heard the voice of desperation. I have sat with forty-year-old women who look seventy. I have blessed children who were wearing their first shoes and first winter coats.

Most of the people who sit down with me are women. It seems that women are more likely to ask for prayer than men. I think it is related to asking for directions when we are lost. We men do not usually do that either.

Sometimes, though, I am surprised.

One year an enormous man wearing a sleeveless jean jacket and sporting tattoos all over his body walked into the armory. He looked like a recently retired small-time professional wrestler. He walked on past me to the medical booth to get his blood pressure checked and his blood sugar level read.

Rather than leaving from there, however, he placed his bag of goods and food box in a corner near the exit and came my way.

"Bless you so much for what you're doin'," he said with a smile on his face but a look in his eyes that conveyed that he had something else on his mind. He continued with a hesitancy in his voice, "I hate takin' help from anyone, but it's been a tough year and my grandkids need things . . . I need stuff, too, I guess. I got diabetes, but I can't afford the medication. They just told me my sugar is over 300 . . . My grandkids really need me. Their dad's in prison for makin' meth, and their mom left town. It's just me, and I don't know what'll happen to 'em if I die."

I knew he wanted prayer but wasn't going to ask. "Can I pray for you?" I offered.

He sat down and bowed his head. I laid my hand on his shoulder. He covered his face with his enormous hand. I prayed. He shook.

When we had finished, he stood up and said, "You just don't know what a blessing this is." Before I knew what was happening, he pulled me into the biggest bear hug I have ever had. I felt like a child in comparison to his size, and I am about six foot two and

215 pounds. He squeezed me for a good ten seconds, an eternity in man-hug time.

He looked at me again and said, "I miss my boy."

The huge wrestler of a father then turned, picked up his bag and food box, and left.

REFLECTION

Nineteenth-century Danish philosopher SØren Kierkegaard wrote, "Ah, how rich was even the neediest person who has ever lived but who still had love compared with the only real pauper, who went through life and never felt a need for anything."*

I was leading a Sunday school class at an old, established downtown church in Austin. On that Sunday, only two were present, an older couple who represented the golden age of that church. They spoke to me of a day when the church was always packed and everyone dressed up for the occasion. The couple was reputed to be the wealthiest household in the church by a long shot.

The scripture for the day was Luke 6:20-26: "Blessed are you who are poor, for yours is the kingdom of God . . . . But woe to you who are rich, for you have received your consolation."

As the woman read the scripture, I could see she was becoming troubled. She said, "We don't fit very well in this story. It seems like we get more of the woes than the blessings."

I responded, "Perhaps we are to stand with the blessed ones—the poor, the hungry, those who weep, and those who are excluded and hated."

The man said, "We really don't know anybody like that."

It then occurred to me that this lovely, well-mannered, philanthropic couple lived a very shielded life. They drove from their stunning house in an exclusive neighborhood, to the country club, to their favorite restaurants, to the opera, and to their church, without ever brushing shoulders with any of those blessed types. For them, evangelism was something done in far-off lands.

Perhaps we have been well fed, well housed, and well heeled, but when we are joined to the body of Christ, we share the needs of a greater body. When we join people who are materially poor in their fight against poverty, we receive their blessings as well. When we listen to them, weep with them, embrace them, and pray with them, we receive a wealth that money can never buy.

If you struggle with seeking Christ for yourself, try seeking him for the sake of another.

QUESTIONS TO CONSIDER

1. Can you remember a time in your life when you experienced a great need? How did it feel?
2. When was the last time you helped a person or people in great need?
3. How did it affect your own relationship with God?

PRAYER CHALLENGE

In the next week, seek out a person in great need. Listen to and pray with this person.

PRAYER

O Lord God, lover of the needy, connect me with the needs of the world. Take me out of my poverty-shielded life and give me compassion for others. Let me meet you where you are at work. In the name of Christ I pray. Amen.

7

lifting the fog

If a brother or sister is poorly clothed and lacking in daily food, and one of you says to them, "Go in peace, be warmed and filled," without giving them the things needed for the body, what good is that? So also faith by itself, if it does not have works, is dead. James 2:15-17

PRAYER ENCOUNTER

The town of Harlan is nestled in the Appalachian Mountains in southeastern Kentucky. Because it is in a low point of the terrain, the fog settles in and stays until about eleven o'clock in the morning.

Our church sets up its clothing tables and stations for distributing food boxes, school supplies, and Bibles, and for offering prayer, in the armory on a Friday afternoon in late October. Then we return the next morning around six thirty and open the doors for distribution half an hour later.

We can gauge the level of need by the line of people that is already there when we arrive. Last year it was one hundred deep on a foggy morning that was about thirty-five degrees and still pitch black. The need was great.

That was the year we decided to offer prayer request cards at the check-in table by the entrance. The idea was that, whether or not people wanted to be prayed with, at least they would be prayed for later.

The armory was filled with people within minutes of our opening the doors. Two hours later, it was still filled. Sue, the coordinator, came to my little prayer and Bible station and handed me a stack of empty prayer request cards. "Paul," she apologized, "They're so focused on getting their food vouchers up there that they can't think about the prayer cards."

Within a minute of the blank cards landing on my table, however, the first one was filled out. Then a line formed to fill out more. Thirty minutes later, I had twenty completed cards. Some of the people filling them out asked me to pray right then and there, and some just handed them to me and said things like, "Prayer is something I surely do need."

I pondered why they had filled out the cards near the exit instead of the entrance. Then I saw three little boys, brothers, I thought. Their small faces were blank. One had patches of missing hair, as if he was undergoing chemo treatment. Another had a bad rash. None of them had warm clothes on. Their hair and skin tone were the same, pale and lusterless. They stood still, silent, and expressionless at the edge of the room.

One of the teenage girls from our youth group began helping them find shoes, then hats, then coats, then gloves. Little by little, as their needs began to be met, the color started coming back into their faces. Next thing I knew, they were chasing each other around the crowded gym. They had become playful children again.

About that time, the fog began to lift, the sun to shine, and the mercury to rise. It was a beautiful day. Then it hit me. When the fog of need settles on people's lives, they cannot see beyond that, beyond their next meal, beyond their cold hands and feet. Only when their needs have been met can people begin to think beyond the moment. That is when we can think to pray, when we become human again.

The exit was a better place for prayer request cards than the entrance, but we must never forget to open the door first and let the people in. The fog will never lift otherwise.

REFLECTION

Not long ago I posted on Facebook, "If you see someone in need, offer to pray with him." The first comment I received was from a young, socially conscious, atheist friend, who can also be a bit of a smart aleck. He wrote, "Why not do something that actually helps the person instead?"

My response to him was, "Prayer is a catalyst for help." I think you would have to really be missing the point if you prayed with a starving man and did not offer him any food.

Origen Adamantius, a third-century Christian scholar and theologian, believed that, in prayer, God connects those who are in need with those who have means. A sick man prays for healing, and at the same time a physician is praying to be useful to the Kingdom of God. God draws the physician to the sick man for healing.

In prayer we are connected through Christ by the Holy Spirit to the whole body of praying souls. Frequently when I have asked God to help a person in need, I hear him saying back to me, "That is why you are here. You help him."

The great church reformer and theologian John Calvin wrote, "Everyone should rather consider that, however great he is, he owes himself to his neighbors, and that the only limit to his aid is the failure of his means."* In other words, the only limit to the help we are to give to another is all that we have.

When we pray for a person to receive help, God gives us responsibility for helping that person to the extent to which we are able. If we are not able on our own, we are to invite others to help. This is the beauty of a faith community. Collectively we are able to help to a much greater extent than any of us could on our own, *if* we are praying for others in need.

Anyone can do good works, but the ones who do them regularly tend to be regularly in prayer for others.

QUESTIONS TO CONSIDER

1. Can you think of a person you could have helped but did not? Why?
2. Have you ever felt helpless to help others?
3. Have you ever been the answer to prayer for someone?

PRAYER CHALLENGE

Pray with a person who needs help. Listen for God to tell you how you should help. Then help.

PRAYER

O God, our help, help me to be a help to others. Direct me to people who need my help. In the name of Christ I pray. Amen.

8

prayer for an "infidel"

I give thanks to my God always for you because of the grace of God that was given you in Christ Jesus. 1 Corinthians 1:4

Prayer Encounter

I put out a message to my Facebook friends, soliciting stories of how prayer has impacted their lives. I was quite surprised when the first to respond was Win. This is the story he shared.

I'm not a Person of Faith—I follow the teachings of Jesus without believing in his divinity. I may have spent many preadult years in the Presbyterian Church, but not all of it stuck.

Not long after we became an "established" couple, Susan had a ruptured disk that eventually required surgery. I was with her at the hospital, and while I was there, she received a visit from the associate pastor of her church. It was a good visit, very pastoral and comforting, and when he took her hand and said, "Let us pray," I stood silently by. As you'd expect, he prayed for comfort and healing—and he gave thanks that I was there to be with her.

I think you could have knocked me over with a feather. Nobody had ever given thanks to their god for my presence, ever. I was both lifted and humbled, a truly astonishing and eye-opening experience. I'm still an infidel, but that was one of the most moving experiences of my life—along with seeing Susan's pain-free smile after successful surgery.

P.S. A couple of years later, that pastor officiated at our wedding.

Not long after I read Win's story, I traveled with members of our church and other churches to Harlan for our annual mission trip. I asked our mission workers to ask everyone who came into the armory to get the food and clothes we had brought if they would like to be prayed for. One man protested, "But not everybody is a believer."

I thought of Win and replied, "What difference does that make?"

REFLECTION

During my freshman year of college, I regularly attended programs at the Baptist Student Union (BSU) right next to the campus. It was well located near the buildings where most of my classes were held. If you were a regular, you could get a parking pass. Also, on Monday nights they had free pizza before the praise service. That, plus some cute Baptist girls, was plenty of reason for me to be a regular at the BSU.

One night they brought in a guest speaker who was one of the higher-ups in the BSU organization. He was to give a how-to talk on evangelism. I was not raised with this sort of talk. It was not until I went through sales training as a financial advisor that I realized that what that man had presented was a standard sales model with Biblical language. It was not a Biblical model of evangelism.

The talk made me very uncomfortable. The motivation the speaker offered was quite simple: If we do not convince people to invite Jesus Christ into their hearts, they will most assuredly go to hell. That is a lot of pressure! My Baptist friends knew all about hell because they had seen a video when they were around eight years old that had scared the hell out of them. That was the only motivation they needed.

But it did not feel right to me. It felt too much like selling some kind of holy insurance.

Later, when I worked as a financial advisor in New York, I always knew when one of my colleagues was selling insurance. Every pitch that wafted over the cubicle walls was peppered with the phrase *God forbid*. God forbid, you were to die. God forbid, your spouse were to die. God forbid, your house were to burn down. God forbid!

The motivator is fear. The salesperson creates anxiety a person perhaps has never had before in order to present a solution for the newfound fear.

Is that evangelism?

God forbid, if you were to die today, what would happen to your soul? I have a great product to show you right now that will ensure its eternal safety.

You may read this and say, "Absolutely! Where do I sign?" But know that many of us would rather have teeth pulled without anesthesia than undergo this kind of sales pitch. God forbid.

Now, I know this style of evangelism has gone the way of eight-track players and New Coke. But much of the North American world still thinks that is what is called evangelism, and it does not want anything to do with it.

Prayer addresses a very deep need that dogma cannot satisfy. We all have come up against circumstances that have put us in a state of helplessness. Prayer connects us and others with the higher power.

What the associate pastor did for Win, my "infidel" friend, was simple and genuine. The pastor recognized Win's worth and presence before Christ in prayer. I call that evangelism.

QUESTIONS TO CONSIDER

1. What comes to mind when you hear the word *evangelism*?
2. Do you consider yourself an evangelist?
3. Have you ever participated in evangelism? How so?

PRAYER CHALLENGE

Think of some of the people you know who do not count themselves as believers. Rather than debating with them, ask them how you might pray for them. What makes them anxious? What do they need? Is there a loved one they are concerned about?

PRAYER

Almighty God, make me a connection between you and those I pray for in the name of Christ. Amen.

9

authentic evangelism

When he was at table with them, he took the bread and blessed and broke it and gave it to them. And their eyes were opened, and they recognized him. And he vanished from their sight. They said to each other, "Did not our hearts burn within us while he talked to us on the road, while he opened to us the Scriptures?" Luke 24:30-32

PRAYER ENCOUNTER

A couple of years ago I was eating at a diner with a retired Baptist pastor. I shared with him that I wanted to learn to be a better evangelist, but I did not quite know how to do it in a way that was authentic to my faith.

Our waitress was a Muslim woman named Nazdar, who, over the months we had been frequenting the restaurant, had shared that she had been ostracized from her community because of the man she had married and later divorced. She and her children had been rejected by their own family.

As she served us, my pastor friend stopped her and said, "Let's have a prayer. Brother Paul will pray for us." Uh-uh. I was caught way off guard. My friend took her hand and mine, and I completed the circle. I knew it is quite against Muslim conduct for a man to touch a woman unless they are married. It all happened so fast, though. Her hand was in mine.

I prayed for Nazdar and her children, I prayed for their safety and for God to meet all their needs, and I prayed in the name of Christ. It only took a moment. As I finished, I could see that she was visibly moved. Tears filled her eyes, and she was flushed.

She said, "As you prayed, I felt a great warmth in my chest. What was that?" I responded, "The Spirit of Christ." She walked off, stunned, and, I believe, changed. She had encountered Christ in a brief moment of prayer in a way that no amount of talking about Christ could have possibly accomplished.

My Baptist friend smiled at me and asked, "Did that feel authentic to your faith?" Indeed, it did! It was as authentic as anything I have ever experienced. It was real. It was not salesy or scripted. It put Nazdar's needs first rather than my own. We all met Christ together.

REFLECTION

Evangelism is a good word, literally. Found throughout the New Testament, the Greek word *euangélion* is translated as "gospel" or "good news" or "good message."

Within the word itself is the word we know as *angel*, which means "messenger." One could say that those who deliver the good news are angels. While I do believe in the nonhuman version of angels within the heavenly realm, I also believe that you and I are angels when we deliver good news.

Perhaps you have had a person come into your life with good news at just the time you needed it. Coincidence? I think not. God sent an angel to you, an evangel.

There is no person on this earth who is not in need of good news. But good news does not look the same to everyone. It depends on each person's need, and everyone has different needs. There is no cookie-cutter approach to evangelism, the delivery of good news.

Do you read any of the mass-distribution marketing letters you receive in the mail? "Dear Current Resident." Do you think,

"Oh my, is this company talking to me? That's me! I am Current Resident." No? I did not think so. I know none of us like phone calls that begin with a bit of dead air followed by an unfamiliar voice asking, "Am I speaking to [insert your name here]?" On the other hand, most of us absolutely love to get letters, cards, phone calls, and even e-mails and texts from people who care about us.

When I was a child, I loved the mail. I could not wait for the postman to deliver it each day. I rarely received anything, but the possibility was always there. I always liked the way my grandparents addressed the envelopes of my birthday cards: Master Paul Burns. *Master* seemed a bit extreme to me, but it made me feel important.

I think the prospect of getting mail thrilled me so much as a child because something in the mail always meant good news. Every card had the potential of containing a check or cold hard cash.

As an adult, I am not quite as enthusiastic about the mail. I get plenty of mail addressed to me, but most of it is junk and the rest are bills or letters from organizations wanting something from me. That is never good news! But every once in a while I receive something special, something just for me, something that requires nothing of me—a gift.

What if evangelizing was less like delivering junk mail or handing someone a bill and more like giving someone a gift from someone who knows each of us better than anyone else can, even better than we know ourselves, a gift from our very creator?

Nazdar received a great gift that day, the presence of Christ, delivered through prayer.

Questions to Consider

1. What is the best news you have ever received?
2. What made the news so good?
3. What good news did Christ deliver and how did he deliver it?

PRAYER CHALLENGE

Pray with someone of a different faith.

PRAYER

O Lord, deliverer of good news to the poor and captive, make the good news of your presence in this world fresh to me again. Make me an angel for others! In Christ's name I pray. Amen.

10

an overheard prayer

Do not neglect to show hospitality to strangers, for thereby some have entertained angels unawares. Hebrews 13:2

PRAYER ENCOUNTER

My good friend Josh had just come back to town, and we met for lunch at our favorite Ethiopian restaurant. While he has actually been to Ethiopia, I just eat the food every now and then.

Josh is very energetic and always comes with fresh stories from his world travels. He works alongside missionaries and helps capture their ministry on video and in photographs. At the same time, I always have some local ministry I am equally passionate about.

As a result, our conversations are usually loud and nonstop. While we talk, I often wonder about how annoying we must be to the other diners, especially in a little restaurant like the one we were in on this particular day.

The restaurant was empty except for me and Josh, a woman sitting by herself, and the owner. Josh struck up a conversation with the owner, and, of course, it turned out that Josh had traveled to this man's hometown, somewhere in Ethiopia. The restaurant was really struggling, and the owner and his wife were barely making it. He was concerned that his faith as a Muslim was hurting his business.

I asked if we could pray for his business and his family. He accepted. We prayed for new customers and blessings for his wife and children. He thanked us graciously and went back to work.

Josh then went to go wash up. Usually I just start loading up my plate at the buffet and stuffing my face. But on this day I stayed seated and waited for Josh to come back, which he soon did.

After a moment or two, the woman, still the only other customer in the place, approached us. She said, "I knew you were Christians when you waited for your friend to come back from the bathroom. You rarely see manners like that anymore." My mother would be so proud.

She continued, "I was really touched when you prayed for the restaurant owner. I work for a retirement home, and it's often depressing. Today has been particularly tough. Your conversation with each other and the way you prayed for that man really made my day."

Josh jumped up out of his seat, exclaiming, "I'll be right back!" He hurried to his car and returned with a stack of Styrofoam-backed posters. The picture was of a beautiful scene near the sea in South Africa. Printed on the posters were words of hope from the Bible.

One of Josh's many side ministries is to turn his photographs into posters and put scripture on them to give to widows. The posters are truly inspiring. He always keeps a stack of them in his trunk.

He said, "Take these back with you and give them to whoever needs them the most." The woman was touched. She took her posters and went to pay her bill. We watched as she showed them to the restaurant owner. He exclaimed, "I have been there! That is my home, my Africa! Where did you get this?"

She explained and gave one to him. He needed it.

REFLECTION

Certain people have a wonderful ability to draw people out of their shells. Yes, they are often extraverts, but more than that they are people-focused extraverts. They do not talk just to hear themselves talk. They listen as well as speak. They create energy and movement everywhere they go.

My friend Josh is such a person. Although some extraverts wear me out, I always leave him with more energy than I started with. I myself am right on the line between introvert and extravert, according to personality tests.

One thing was for sure; the woman who approached us in the restaurant was an introvert. It took everything she had to walk over to our table to talk with us. Taking that leap changed her day and another person's day as well. And who knows how many more days were changed after she went back to work at the retirement home?

When I share my thoughts on prayer with others, introverts cringe. This is an activity best left to extraverts, some say. But this prayer encounter thing is not as hard or as scary as you might imagine.

We all have these bubbles around us. The bubble is our space, our goings-on. We stay in our bubble, and others stay in theirs. But most bubbles are not ironclad. They pop so very easily. Just a small gesture can dissolve a person's bubble and lead to a connection being made. A little eye contact and a word about the season ("Got your Christmas shopping done?"), or the weather ("How about this pretty day?"), or the food ("The ribs are really good here."). Perhaps the person is reading a book ("Do you recommend it?").

A person who is not open to talking will communicate that. But whether you live up north, down south, out west, or back east, very few people will be offended by the asking.

I learned this by watching my dad. He is essentially an introvert who makes a very intentional effort to connect with people. If we are in line at the theater, he always manages to strike up some kind of conversation with someone next to us. It is not that it comes naturally to him, but he believes it is valuable to explore the connections of our humanity.

You never know what kind of special person you might meet by leaving your bubble. You never know what kind of impact you might make.

I heard a story on one of the morning news shows about a Secret Santa who travels around the country every December and passes out hundred dollar bills to people he feels led to. Although his identity remains anonymous, he allows a journalist to follow him and record some of what goes on.

This past Christmas he found a young man in a train station and gave him one hundred dollars. The man was in tears. He kept repeating, "This is amazing! This is amazing!"

The news story reported that the man was a struggling heroin addict who did not believe in God. He had failed his wife and his child. He had not held a job in a year. They were losing their house. One hundred dollars would not change that. However, the day before, his wife had begged him to pray, even if he did not believe. "Just throw one up. It's a start." He did. He asked for God's help and a sign of his existence.

He got it in the form of a stranger in a red Santa hat who gave him one hundred dollars and prayed with him. He has entered a rehab program. Not for the first time, but, he said, "The first time with the help of a higher power."

There are angels out there. Perhaps you are one.

QUESTIONS TO CONSIDER

1. Have you spoken with a stranger recently? How did it affect your day?
2. If you believed that just by talking with people you could make the world a better place, why would you hold back?
3. Can you think of a time when a stranger made your day better or perhaps even changed your life?

PRAYER CHALLENGE

Pray with a stranger. You cannot force this. The need and receptiveness have to be there. The key is to be open to having encounters with strangers and to trust the leading of the Spirit.

Paul M. Burns

PRAYER

O Lord, you welcomed me as a stranger and made me a friend. Call me out of my shell and use me to confirm your existence to another. In Jesus' name I pray. Amen.

11

prayer hungry

You're blessed when you've worked up a good appetite for God. He's food and drink in the best meal you'll ever eat.
Matthew 5:6*

PRAYER ENCOUNTER

Have you ever woken up with a huge appetite? The kind where you feel like you could take on Paul Bunyan in a flapjack-eating contest? I awoke with a hunger like this for prayer on a day that I was to be the pastor for the day at Siloam Family Health Center, a low-cost medical-care provider for the refugee and immigrant population in Nashville.

Prayer at Siloam is a team effort. The standard procedure is for employees to ask all of the patients if they would like the pastor for the day to pray for them. The pastor prays for about half a dozen people every day. That, however, would not be nearly enough for the appetite the Lord was giving me on this day. The number that came to my mind was forty.

I do not tell this story to lift myself up in any way but to share how satisfying praying with others can be. I wish I woke up hungry like this every day, but usually I am more interested in flapjacks.

Siloam's employees and volunteers for the day gather for prayer every morning before they open the doors. What a great place to work! They pray for God to be seen through their work and that they themselves might see him at work.

On this particular day, everyone was tired. They had held a big donor event the day before for which they had been planning for months. When I introduced our mission for the day of praying for forty people, their eyes brightened in spite of their weariness. One of the volunteers who has a remarkably keen sense of the presence of God wondered aloud, "Why do I feel like God is going to rain down fire from Heaven today?"

I suggested that I start with praying for each of them. A line of employees and volunteers formed at the pastoral office door to be prayed for. Because Siloam tracks the number of people who receive prayer, I started the day's log with the names of those I had just prayed for. Then they began sending patients my way.

I used just about every translator Siloam has. We prayed in Arabic, Spanish, Korean, and Chinese. I prayed with Kenyans, Burmese, Iraqis, Mexicans, Chinese, and Croatians. I prayed with the CEO and the head of medicine. We prayed in the lobby, the kids' play area, examining rooms, offices, and even the billing station. We prayed for healing, hope, citizenship, jobs, and loved ones separated by distance but not by spirit.

I can still see many of their faces. I remember a mother and a daughter from Sudan who had lost contact with the rest of their family after being sent to different refugee camps. As I prayed for the lost family members, the mother squeezed my hand and wept.

A young man from China had brought his mother. She had Alzheimer's disease. We talked for a while in the waiting area, and he asked if I would pray for his mother. I took her hand and prayed. A faint smile crossed her face.

One of the employees was leaving after work to go to be with her fiancé whom she had not seen in two months. She asked for prayers of blessing for their relationship and wedding plans.

One patient suffered greatly from depression and loneliness. I sat and listened to her. As we prayed, she took both my hands. I heard the faint sound of her own murmured pleas as I prayed for her. After I said Amen, she smiled up at me and asked, "Can I give you a hug?"

With an hour to go, I needed to pray with twelve more people to get to forty. Laurie, the occupational therapist, saw that I was starting to tire. She grabbed me and began going up to employees, volunteers, and patients, telling them, "You need prayer! Let's pray!" By the time the hour was up, we had made it to forty-six.

I came home stuffed full of something much better than even flapjacks—the Spirit. I was exhausted and satiated at the same time. I dozed off remembering all the stories and faces I had heard and seen and how the Spirit had indeed rained down upon us from heaven.

REFLECTION

This past year I had the privilege of spending a week at a retreat center in North Carolina. I have benefited greatly from weeks like this, though it always takes me most of the week just to shut things down. I go through cell phone and computer withdrawal, even wristwatch withdrawal. But by the end of the week, I am usually unwound enough to really pray.

Midway through that week, I was finally starting to relax a bit. I had stopped thinking about the last church committee meeting and the broken men's room toilet. My cell phone was turned off and tucked away in my luggage.

As I sat quietly on an oversized loveseat with a coffee table in front of me, I imagined a huge feast spread out across the table, a spiritual feast. It occurred to me that this feast is always before me if I would just partake of it.

Most of the time, I go from task to task and then head home and crash in front of the TV. Meanwhile, my spirit is starving. Can you relate?

Before us at any time is a spiritual feast ready for the eating, but often we are not hungry for it. It is kind of like when you get hooked on junk food and an apple does not interest you at all, even if it might be the best thing for you and one of the most wonderful foods there is.

A few years ago I went on the Atkins diet. For a month I ate nothing but meat and veggies, very little carbs and nothing sweet. The first fruits you are allowed to reintroduce to your diet are berries, then melons, then apples. I remember when I had that first bite of fruit. It was miraculous! It was as if I had never before had fruit in my life, it was so sweet and good. My body craved it, needed it.

What our spirit craves more than anything is to commune with God, and this is possible by prayer. First, though, we must remove all of the spiritual junk food in our lives.

Turn off your phone, your computer, your TV. The world will go on without your attention for a little bit. The true feast will begin to emerge. Dine.

QUESTIONS TO CONSIDER

1. Do you ever go a day having without your phone with you?
2. When was the last time you spent more than ten minutes in prayer?
3. What whets your spiritual appetite?

PRAYER CHALLENGE

Set aside a whole day without any electronics and devote it to spiritual activity. Take a Bible, a journal perhaps, maybe even a picnic basket, and find a retreat. This does not mean that you have to say words of prayer all day. Just keep the line open with God. Let him refresh and feed you.

PRAYER

Lord, give me a hunger for your presence. Make me lie down in green pastures. Lead me beside still waters. Restore my soul. Prepare a table before me and anoint me. Amen.

12

praying for angel

May the God of hope fill you with all joy and peace in believing,
so that by the power of the Holy Spirit you may abound in hope.
Romans 15:13

PRAYER ENCOUNTER

There may not be a more anxious place than a hospital's neonatal intensive care unit (NICU), as I discovered the summer I served as a chaplain in one to complete an ordination requirement. Some NICU stories do not end well. Then there is the story of a baby who was born at twenty-five weeks, Angel, a tiny boy whose name evoked those heavenly beings who must have been watching over him.

At twenty-five weeks, the lungs are not ready to breathe on their own. Baby Angel had a breathing tube and a feeding tube, and the nurses kept him in an incubator. They had to regularly put ointment on him because at that age the skin is not quite ready for exposure to the air.

His mother spoke very little English. The first time I met her, I had a translator with me. I prayed for the baby and for her.

After the initial visit, I did not need a translator. Angel's mother knew who I was and why I was there. I would pray, and she would make the sign of the cross.

I did not always see her, though her name was on the visitor check-in sheet every day without fail. On those days, I would stand by Angel's incubator, pray silently, and watch him fighting for his life. I remember that tiny little chest working so hard. He was red all over and peeling as if he had a bad sunburn.

Some days the doctors were hopeful, some days they were not.

Around week thirty, Angel's mother told me she wanted Angel to be baptized. She was Catholic, but she had not been to Mass in years and did not know a priest. She asked if I would do it. I was honored.

Angel's mother, her husband, her mother, her sister, a translator, a nurse, and myself crowded around the incubator. We prayed while holding hands. I read some scripture and asked the Spirit to descend upon the dropperful of water. I was not allowed to touch Angel because of the delicacy of his skin.

I reached my gloved hand into the incubator and held the dropper of blessed water above his tiny head covered with a mass of dark hair. "I baptize you, Angel, in the name of the Father" (drip), "and of the Son" (drip), "and of the Holy Spirit" (drip). "Amen." I prayed for God's protection and for further growth of both body and spirit.

There were tears all around. In those tears were hope (drip), anxiety (drip), and love (drip).

The daily visits and prayers continued. Then I got a call.

It was my last week at the hospital. Angel had been born a few weeks before I arrived that summer. It had been eleven weeks of praying for him. My heart beat fast as I picked up the phone. Most calls from the NICU were not good.

Angel's mother and father were at the NICU, and they wanted to see me. It was Angel's last day in the hospital.

I entered the room where the family awaited me. They said the only thing they knew I would understand, "Gracias!" as they handed the living and healthy Angel to me. I held him with my own hands and said, "Gracias, O Dios!"

I baptized him again, with my tears (drip) (drip) (drip).

REFLECTION

In 2007 my wife, Jennifer, and I moved to Nashville. I had been called as the pastor of Priest Lake Presbyterian Church, an adventure I could not have anticipated. Sometime in my first few months there, two men from Gideons International came to introduce themselves and welcome me to the community.

I had been a pastor long enough to know that most people who visit you unannounced want something from you, but not Jeff and Woody. Yes, they had an agenda, but they put it aside. They sat down with me and listened to me talk about how my ministry was going and how Jennifer was adjusting to this new and crazy life.

I must admit that I was somewhat guarded with them. After all, they were strangers. Then they asked if they could pray for me. I agreed. It was not a generic prayer. They had really listened to me carefully. They remembered my name and my wife's name. They used the name of my church. They prayed for all of the concerns and hopes I had talked about.

In all honesty, I could not remember when I had been prayed for like that in my life. I felt truly blessed and cared for by these men.

If that one-time visit and prayer had been it, I would have been forever grateful to them. But it did not end there. Every year men from the Gideons visit me, though not always the same ones. They must have a file on me or something because they always allude to the former prayer requests and ask how those things are going. I feel as if I have angels.

After a few years, Woody asked if he might give a brief presentation on the mission of the Gideons at our worship service. I was kind of reluctant to let him. Perhaps it would not match our mission and theology. I really did not know what I was worried about, but I was uneasy when I told him yes. We put a date on the calendar.

Woody called a month out to confirm, but there was a conflict. We put another date on the calendar, but there was another conflict. I am ashamed to say that I canceled on him three times over the period of a year. However, that was an unusual year.

First, during the summer of that year, I felt strongly that God was calling our church to pay off our two mortgages. We were struggling greatly to make these payments, and they had been refinanced multiple times. Enough was enough. Guess who was praying for our campaign? Woody. We are now debt free.

In February the next year, the unthinkable happened. A tornado all but destroyed our sanctuary. Guess who was praying for us as we rebuilt? Woody.

That August we rededicated our renovated sanctuary and celebrated our thirtieth anniversary as a church. Guess who prayed for this celebration? Woody.

Woody had a new date on the calendar for the first Sunday after Labor Day. This time I did not cancel. He stood up, a stranger to all but me, and recited the history of his prayers for our church. The congregation was blown away and utterly moved. He spoke for only five minutes and then showed a short video about the Gideons' mission. Then he prayed for us once again.

It is a wonderful thing to be prayed for over and over again, to have someone out there who is sharing in your joys and sorrows, who is hoping for your hopes.

QUESTIONS TO CONSIDER

1. Can you think of a period in your life that was like what Angel's parents went through? What gave you hope?
2. Have you ever had someone pray for you like the Gideons did for me? How did it make you feel?
3. Do you know someone who is going through a difficult time?

PRAYER CHALLENGE

Ask God to lead you to a person who is in need of your ongoing prayers. Begin praying for and with that person.

PRAYER

God of unending faithfulness and care, lead me to a person who needs my continuing prayers. Help me to be a good listener. Let me share that person's joys, sorrows, and hopes. In the name of our great intercessor, Christ, I pray. Amen.

13

janelle's dilemma

Let us then with confidence draw near to the throne of grace, that we may receive mercy and find grace to help in time of need. Hebrews 4:16

PRAYER ENCOUNTER

I got a call from the nurse's station in the antepartum unit. Antepartum is where they put expectant mothers who require bed rest and medical supervision. It is a difficult place to be.

The call was about a fifteen-year-old girl who was twenty weeks pregnant with triplets. She had preeclampsia, which is a condition that can emerge during pregnancy that puts a mother at risk of both stroke and liver and kidney damage. More often than not, it can be managed with bed rest and proper medical care. It goes away after the baby has been delivered.

Janelle's condition was very serious. Her blood pressure indicated that she could have a stroke at any time, and her kidneys were on the verge of failure. The babies within her were healthy, but they would need to spend at least twenty-three weeks in gestation to have any chance of survival at all. She would never make it three more weeks in her condition.

Her doctor recommended aborting the triplets to save Janelle's life. Her pastor and her parents did not approve. Janelle was not talking to any of them.

The situation had thrown the doctor and the nurses into a panic. The doctor was furious with Janelle's parents and distraught over Janelle. A nurse told me over the phone, "We need a chaplain down here to pray with this girl."

I had visited with Janelle a few times over the previous week. When I first met her, she was working on a *Little Mermaid* coloring book. I had even met the father of the babies, a scared, skinny boy no more than sixteen years old. I had never seen Janelle's parents or her pastor.

I walked into the room, and Janelle refused to make eye contact with me. She would not talk. Her face was closed, and her jaw was clenched. Fifteen-year-old girls should not be lying in this part of a hospital having to make a decision like this.

I sat down and asked her if she understood the seriousness of her condition. No response. I told her that she could have a stroke at any time. Nothing.

I knew I should pray, but for the life of me I could not figure out how. Should I pray that she decide to have an abortion against her family's and her own conscience? Should I pray for God to heal her condition? But I had been doing that for the last week!

As I pulled up a chair to her bedside, I prayed silently for direction. Nothing. So I asked if she would give me her hand, and I just started praying out loud about the unfairness of Janelle's dilemma. Then the words came, "Lord, take this decision away from Janelle!"

Janelle squeezed my hand tightly. Tears escaped from her eyes. Her dilemma was in God's hands now.

It was Friday. I had to get back home to Austin, a long three-hour commute. I prayed off and on during the drive, reminding myself that I had put it all in God's hands.

I returned to the hospital the next Monday and found a note from the weekend chaplain: "Visit room 703. 15-year-old girl. Miscarriage. Triplets. Friday, 10:05 p.m."

I entered the room with no idea what to expect. Janelle was a teenager again, chatting away on the phone with a girlfriend. Her mother was with her, straightening up the room. Her pastor had just left. The dilemma was gone.

Janelle held up a picture of three tiny babies in blue with little warm hats and said, "Aren't they cute? They look like they're sleeping."

They were. In God's hands.

REFLECTION

At some point in each of our lives we will be confronted by an impossible decision.

Abraham was faced with just such a decision in Genesis 22. The Lord commanded him to sacrifice Isaac, the son that he and his wife, Sarah, had been promised for so long. It is a story that today baffles and confuses most of us who read it. Why would God ask for such a sacrifice?

Dutifully following God's instructions, Abraham told his servants to stay with the donkey that had brought them to Mount Moriah and assured them that he and the boy would return after they had worshipped further on. Did he mean this? Did he really have confidence that he would return with Isaac? I believe so. I believe Abraham fully intended to follow God's command, and he trusted that somehow God would deliver his son at the same time.

Abraham then led Isaac up the mountain, with wood for fire and a knife to do the deed. The biblical text tells us nothing of Abraham's emotions or thoughts, but he must have gone through great turmoil. As he held the knife above his son, an angel of the Lord intervened and stopped him, praising him for his faithfulness. A ram appeared, and a more suitable sacrifice was made. Abraham returned with the boy.

Janelle, though only a teenager, fully believed that it would be wrong to abort her babies. It was what she had been told, and she accepted this. Whether you or I agree with her decision or not, she stuck with her convictions at the risk of her own life.

Sometimes we just have to walk up that mountain, approach the throne of grace, and trust that God is merciful. He is, and he will be.

Questions to Consider

1. Have you ever been faced with a lose—lose circumstance? What did you do?
2. What kind of decisions do you pray about?
3. Do you know someone who is faced with a difficult decision?

Prayer Challenge

Pray with someone who has a difficult decision to make. Ask God to lead that person through it.

Prayer

O merciful Lord, show me a person who is trapped between a rock and a hard place. Allow me to be a support and intercessor in prayer for that person. In the name of the most holy sacrifice, Jesus Christ, I pray. Amen.

14

the night of the fire

But Jesus looked at them and said, "With man this is impossible, but with God all things are possible." Matthew 19:26

PRAYER ENCOUNTER

While working as a chaplain at the hospital in Dallas, I experienced something that opened me up more fully to the possibilities of the miraculous power of Christ.

Throughout my summer there, I spent much time listening to patients and offering prayer. I spent most of my time with mothers and fathers in the NICU. I ministered to thirty-two mothers who had lost babies. Often I just sat and wondered what in the world I had to offer. I usually felt helpless.

I read Psalm 46 over and over, "God is our refuge and strength, a very present help in trouble." I did not really understand it, and I was beginning to wonder how true it was. I prayed for comfort. But I had no miracle prayers to offer. Nothing and no one would bring those babies back.

One night while I was on call, something horrible happened. A homeless man who had been admitted earlier in the day tried to light a cigarette while wearing an oxygen mask. He blew up the tank. He died later that night.

The fire threw the whole hospital into chaos. I went from floor to floor, helping in whatever way I could, but mainly I just tried not to add to the confusion. As I approached the NICU, I heard weeping in the waiting room. Not your standard sniff—sniff sort of crying but something more like a heart-wrenching wail. The kind that you can feel in your core.

I entered the room and found a young couple, a man holding a woman as she rocked back and forth, sobbing. In the midst of the fire's turmoil, they had received terrible news: their newborn baby had a severe brain bleed. The MRI revealed damage that could not be repaired. Perhaps the child would live a few years but with severe problems.

The thought that entered my head was, "*No!* Not this time!" I sat with the couple and cried out to God for healing in a way that I never had before. I had never really prayed for physical healing until now. That had always felt too risky to me. What if healing did not happen? What would that do to someone's faith?

A few days later, as I was scrubbing up before entering the NICU, a young man, face beaming, came bounding up to me. "Chaplain? Do you remember me?"

I did. It was the young man who had held his distraught wife in the waiting room.

"I'm so glad I found you. Thank you for your prayer! The next morning they did another scan of our baby's brain, and there was no bleeding and no damage! They held up the two scans and pointed out where the damage had been and where it was gone. The doctor couldn't explain it. Yesterday we found a church and gave our lives to Christ!"

He could not have delivered better news to me.

I was still a bit doubtful, though. It could have been just a mistake.

I usually attended the morning check-in, and I made a point to be at the next one. The baby's doctor was there. It was a doctor I normally avoided. He always seemed angry. When I prayed with a family, he generally looked as if he felt uncomfortable and usually found an excuse to leave the room.

When we got to the chart for the miracle baby, he just said, "This one's going home today. Brain function is healthy. No more bleeding." I tried to interject with a question, but he just glared at me and moved on.

I knew what had happened to that baby, however, and I chose to believe it. Believing opened up something inside of me, a possibility that I had not really considered: *All things are possible for God.*

REFLECTION

A few years ago I was leading a Sunday school class comprised of some very intelligent and well-meaning Christians. We were studying Luke 18:35-43, which describes one of the many miraculous healings of Jesus. A blind man was made to see!

A discussion about belief in miracles ensued, spurred on by a rather strange and somewhat disruptive visitor. Outside of the visitor, the general opinion of the class was that miracles are simply an old-world misunderstanding. Over time, the class decided, enough knowledge of the physical world would wash away the superstitious and ignorant belief in miracles.

The visitor, though, kept pressing the others on the possibility of miracles. Hoping to make some peace, I asked, "What would it cost us to believe in miracles?" The class looked at me, puzzled. The odd visitor replied, "Your dignity. You would lose your dignity. People would think you were out of your mind."

The question and the visitor's answer to it really hit the class smack-dab in the face. They were more concerned with rational dignity than with being foolish enough to believe that miracles actually exist. Sure, we always hear reports of miracles over in Africa and places where education is poor, but in the "civilized" world, we know better.

Or perhaps miracles happen in such areas as those because of the great need for them. Perhaps only those people who are in great need ask for miracles. Where there is no water, miracles are needed. Where there are no hospitals, miracles are needed. Where there is no justice, miracles are needed. Where there is palpable evil, miracles are needed.

I recently met a pastor from Haiti named Actionnel Fleurisma. He told me how Christ came to his village.

Actionnel was one of ten children, three of whom died before reaching adulthood. He was raised in a two-room thatched house with a dirt floor. Finding dinner was the daily task of the entire family. The village had no hospital and no school. If you had any kind of problem, physical or spiritual, you had to pay a witch doctor for help. In addition to his fee per visit, everyone had to pay an annual tribute fee to him on Christmas out of fear of being cursed for the coming year. Actionnel described it as a form of slavery.

His mother became deathly ill, and so his father sent for the witch doctor. They paid to have ten dogs and a slew of chickens sacrificed, but it did not help. The witch doctor said the family had done it wrong, so they would have to pay again. Since they had no more money, the witch doctor left.

They needed a miracle.

About the time the witch doctor left, a Christian woman came walking into the village singing the old hymn "There Is Power in the Blood." Actionnel described her presence as having "the smell of hope." She entered the tiny dwelling and prayed for his mother in the name of Christ. His mother was healed. Thirty years later, she still lives. She became the first Christian in the village.

Actionnel was called to ministry when he was in his mid-twenties. He came to America for seminary education. He returned to Haiti and founded a church. This church sent a member to be educated as a doctor. He started a hospital. The church sent young men and women to be educated as teachers, and the church started a school. Many of the witch doctors have become Christians and no longer financially enslave the villagers.

Miracles still happen. This story represents the Good News alive and in action. There is still power in the blood of Christ.

Many of us who are fortunate enough to live in America do not need a miracle for daily survival. If we are sick, we go see a doctor. If we are thirsty, we turn on the faucet. If you have the luxury to read this book, your basic needs are probably being met.

But I contend that we do need the miraculous, and that miracles do happen, even in America in the twenty-first century.

QUESTIONS TO CONSIDER

1. Have you experienced or witnessed the miraculous? Do share!
2. Do you pray for miracles? Why or why not?
3. What difference for you does it make to believe in miracles?

PRAYER CHALLENGE

Do not hold back! Pray for the impossible for someone who is in need of it.

PRAYER

O wonderful, working God, instill in me a belief in your power. Allow me to witness and experience your miraculous deeds. Give me faith enough to ask for what is impossible. In the name of the great healer, Christ Jesus my Lord, I pray. Amen.

15

this holy mother

And the angel answered her, "The Holy Spirit will come upon you, and the power of the Most High will overshadow you; therefore the child to be born will be called holy—the Son of God. And behold, your relative Elizabeth in her old age has also conceived a son, and this is the sixth month with her who was called barren. For nothing will be impossible with God." And Mary said, "Behold, I am the servant of the Lord; let it be to me according to your word." And the angel departed from her. Luke 1:35-38

PRAYER ENCOUNTER

One afternoon near the end of my shift, I got a call from one of the nurses in the NICU about a couple requesting a baptism for their baby boy. Ideally baptisms should happen in a church where they can be shared with the whole church family. A baptism is a time of celebration and renewal for the congregation as well as for the person being baptized. But real life has no ideals, only truth. It would be foolish and callous to tell this couple how and where baptisms should happen.

A nurse led me into a partitioned corner of the NICU where a small gathering awaited me in silence. Present were the mother, the father, and the sister and the aunt of the mother. The baby was lying in a little hospital crib, swaddled tight.

The nurse had warned me before we entered that the baby had been born with severe deformities, most of which were covered by the blanket. All that could be seen was his face, which could only be described as an approximation of a face. It had two eyes, a mouth, and a nose, but it was clearly not what a face should be.

He would not live long. The faces present reflected this fact. The event was an approximation of a joyful event but clearly was not joyful.

The nurse introduced me, and they all nodded toward me. I said the necessary words of scripture and tradition. I prayed for the presence of the Holy Spirit. Water was sprinkled, the child's name, José, was pronounced in the name of the Father and of the Son and of the Holy Spirit. Amen. Then I prayed for the baby and his family.

As I looked up at the mother, I saw something had changed. Her face was alive, her eyes were bright. The father smiled. The mother's sister and aunt hugged each other. It was like watching sleepwalkers awaken. The family had become a family. There was connection.

The mother had said nothing during the baptism except for numb responses to my questions. But now she approached and spoke to me. "Pastor, I would very much like for you to visit me tomorrow. I need to talk."

The next day I found her sitting with her baby in her lap. Her eyes were transfixed on him.

"How are you today?" I asked with concern.

"I'm doing much better." She smiled.

"How's José?"

"He's keeping me and my husband together," she said in an almost cheerful voice.

"Tell me more about that," I answered, a bit disturbed.

"Well, we used to get into it a lot. Then we realized that every time we got into it, José would get worse. So now we don't fight anymore."

"You're saying that your fighting makes your baby sick?"

"Yeah. It's like he wants us to stay together."

"When you say 'he' do you mean God or José?"

As I said this, her face darkened and she visibly winced, though she never broke her gaze with the face of her child. "I don't really like to talk about God. It's hard for me."

"Can you tell me a little more about that?" I asked, very carefully.

"God has done a lot of bad things to me in my life." Now there was a hint of anger in her voice.

Let me stop right here and say that it took all I had to not interrupt this poor woman and explain that God could not have done any bad things to her. I knew just enough to know that you cannot talk anyone out of a particular view of God in the midst of trauma, nor should you.

"I know this might be difficult, and I'd understand if you don't want to talk about it, but will you tell me more?"

She continued to stare into her baby's eyes. "When I was eight, my uncle molested me. When I tried to tell my mother, she punished me for making up lies about her brother. When I turned fifteen, my *quinceañera*, he made sexual comments to me. I knew it was no good to tell my mother. When I was seventeen, I got pregnant. My mother kicked me out of the house. I got arrested for drugs, and I went to prison, where I had my first baby. The state took him away. God's done a lot of bad things to me."

I was silent and stunned. I was angry with her uncle and her mother. I wanted to call the police and see those two behind bars.

"Are you mad at God for what has happened to you?"

"Yes," she stated boldly, as if lightening might strike but she did not care. "Because God does everything that happens. He tests us. I know that he never gives anybody more than they can handle, but I feel like he gave me more than I could take." She paused and gazed even more deeply into José's eyes, and a smile appeared on her face. "Lately, though, I am changing a little about God."

"How so?" I sat as still as I could so that she would continue to talk.

"God did not have to give me any time at all with José. God could have taken José whenever he wanted, but he has given me time with my baby."

After she said these words, she kissed his face, a face only a mother could love, but, oh, how she loved him! It was the most beautiful picture I have ever seen. Love filled her face and poured out upon her son, who was perfected in her eyes. If I were an artist, I would have painted this Holy Mother and Child. I wish you could see it. I still can.

No, this was not the ideal. This was not how life should happen, but it happened.

I asked her if I might give thanks for this precious moment. She nodded, still smiling at her boy, her joy, her salvation. I prayed.

REFLECTION

The last two prayer encounter stories, the one you have just read and the one in the previous chapter where a baby was miraculously healed, both involve infants who were not given much chance of survival. I prayed for healing for both. One lived, and the other died. Why?

This is a question that has led many people to question the existence of a loving, powerful God. Why do babies die? Why do floods destroy whole communities? Why do people who live healthy lifestyles get terminal illnesses? Why, if God is all-powerful and all-loving, does he allow these things to happen? Do miracles really happen, or do we just live in a world of chance?

I cannot answer any of these questions, but I do believe with all my being that miracles happen. Perhaps it will be helpful if I share what I believe a miracle is.

It is a miracle when the transcendent, above and beyond God, becomes immanent, close, and involved. The primary miracle of the Christian faith is Jesus Christ. He is God in the flesh.

Rather than staying above and beyond the human sphere of suffering, God was born in an animal trough, lived among humanity, and died a criminal's death. Along the way to the cross, he healed hundreds, if not thousands, announcing the presence of the Kingdom of God. The Kingdom of God is at hand! It is brought near in Christ.

Therefore, miracles are not exceptions to the natural world but the ever-present reality of the Kingdom of God where Christ is present and reigns. The miraculous is more real than the physical world we know. It is eternal, while the earthly reality is death. A miracle is heaven spilling out into our mundane reality.

Miracles give us hope and a hunger for what is to come.

The difficulty many of us have with miracles is that we have no control over them. We cannot make them happen. They are not magic. Miracles are not just getting what we want. They happen according to the will of God.

Miracles offend our idea of fairness. When one person in a coma awakens and another does not, we are afraid to call one a miracle because it does not seem fair. We desire consistency and predictability. That is the basis of all natural law: predictability. When something is perfectly predictable, it can become a tool that can be grasped and used. God, however, cannot be controlled.

But God does listen. God does see. God does respond.

If a miracle is not just getting what we want but is God being immanent, close, and involved, then perhaps we experience the miraculous more often than we can know, even when we do not get the desired outcome of our prayers.

To me, what happened to the mother whose deformed baby would not live was as much a miracle as the baby in the previous chapter whose brain bleed mysteriously disappeared. God came near to this woman. He made himself present to her through her dying child. She had never stopped believing that God existed, but she had lost faith in his goodness. It was restored. This is a miracle of the highest order, for it is lasting. It is a miracle that God can restore the faith of a woman who was experiencing, without question, something purely tragic.

Today I remember this story whenever I hear about people around the world who are suffering atrocities, and I have hope that

God can and will reach them. And I have to remain open that God may desire to use me to do it.

We are not promised that we will never die. Even that healed baby will die someday, though hopefully decades from now. In fact, we have been told that we must die to receive eternal life. We must die to a life that promises only death.

When we pray, we open ourselves up to the source of all life— and anything can happen, anything!

And Mary said, "Behold, I am the servant of the Lord; let it be to me according to your word."

QUESTIONS TO CONSIDER

1. Can you remember a time in your life when you struggled with your faith? Why? What restored it?
2. Can you think of a time in your life when you knew that God was real?
3. Was it a good time or a hard time?

PRAYER CHALLENGE

Pray with someone who has suffered a great loss. Pray for God to draw near through Christ and that the person you are praying for might know God is real.

PRAYER

O Lord God, Immanuel, God with us, let me encounter your loving presence in my life that I may share it with others. In the name of Jesus Christ, the closeness of God, I pray. Amen.

16

a prayer resolution

I have often heard and said the expression *I'll keep you in my prayers.*
We lead busy lives, and this kind sentiment serves us well in a pinch.
It is a way of saying that not only do we care, but at some point we
will actually do something to show it.

Some people I know have exemplary personal prayer lives. They
arise early and pour over long lists of people and their needs. When
they say, "I'll keep you in my prayers," you can rest assured that you
will be prayed for.

I suspect, however, that most people are more like me. I am very
inconsistent in my personal prayer life. I am guilty many times over
of saying that I will pray for someone and then forgetting to do it.

One day my guilt finally caught up with me, and I decided to
make a change. I remembered something a since-passed saint of the
church did with me more than a few times. If I asked him to pray
for something, he would immediately start praying. It did not matter
if we were on the phone, in a restaurant, or on the golf course with
an impatient foursome behind us. He would drop everything and
pray with me.

So, I made a resolution to never say I would pray for someone
at a later time. Instead, I would always offer to pray right then and
there. I am not saying that I never pray later for that person as well.

In fact, I have found that I am much more likely to pray later when I also pray now.

Since making that resolution, I have found myself praying for people in all kinds of places. Sometimes it is a bit awkward at first, but it always seems to have a great effect.

There is something about praying with someone that is so very powerful and cannot be replaced by a promise of prayer or even a word of care. It is the difference between telling someone what you are having for dinner tonight and actually extending an invitation to come over and eat it with you.

Jesus said, "Behold, I stand at the door and knock. If anyone hears my voice and opens the door, I will come in to him and eat with him, and he with me" (Rev. 3:20). When we pray with someone, we are sharing a meal with Jesus. The potential in this meal is so much greater than anything you and I could ever offer without him.

Prayer is a powerful form of evangelism. There is something about prayer that disarms people. For me, prayer has become the most authentic way to share Christ with others.

One of the most influential things I read during my seminary education was John Calvin's description of the Lord's Supper. Calvin believed that, although it is physically impossible for the body of Jesus to be literally present on altars across the world, Christ is indeed truly present in the meal.

Calvin believed that, by the power of the Holy Spirit, those with faith are lifted into the presence of Jesus Christ, who resides in heaven at the right hand of the Father. Like on *Star Trek*, our spirits are beamed up before the Lord, who feeds us with grace by his own hand.

It is my belief that the same thing happens when we pray: the Spirit transports our spirits before Christ in heaven. Prayer beams us up to Christ. When we pray, we are very much being lifted in spirit into the presence of our God.

This encounter can change us forever.

F. B. Meyer, one of the great preachers of the early twentieth century, wrote, "The great tragedy of life is not unanswered prayer, but unoffered prayer."* Without prayer, we have no more relationship with God than we do with the president. We may hear about him and even talk about him, but we do not know him.

If prayer is the way we pursue a relationship with God, then it can also be a way we can share our relationship with God with others. Rather than talking to others about the God we know through Christ and what he can do for their lives, why not take them directly to Christ through prayer?

Prayer is certainly not the only way we encounter Christ; but it is a practice and we need practices. We need concrete actions that we can do, like a sacrament, to administer the grace of Christ to this needful world. We can join him in changing the world one prayer at a time!

Make a prayer resolution for your life and prepare yourself for the encounter of a lifetime.

PRAYER

Lord, encounter me as I pray. Break into my life and share with me the life that lasts. Help me to boldly go where perhaps no others have gone before, and pray with others. In the name of Christ I pray. Amen.

notes

All scripture passages, with the exception of Matthew 5:6 in chapter 11, come from *The Holy Bible, English Standard Version; Containing the Old and New Testaments* (Wheaton, IL: Crossway Bibles, 2001).

Chapter 6
    Søren Kierkegaard, *Works of Love,* trans. Howard V. Hong and Edna H. Hong (Princeton, NJ: Princeton University Press, 1995), 10.

Chapter 7
    John Calvin, *Institutes of the Christian Religion,* trans. Henry Beveridge (Grand Rapids, MI: Wm. B. Eerdmans, 1989), 3.7.13.

Chapter 11
    Eugene H. Peterson, *Conversations: The Message with Its Translator* (Colorado Springs, CO: NavPress, 2007), 1491.

Chapter 16
    John Blanchard, comp., *Gathered Gold: A Treasury of Quotations for Christians* (Durham, UK: Evangelical Press, 1984), 231.

about the author

Paul Burns serves as the pastor of Priest Lake Presbyterian Church in Nashville, Tennessee. He holds an MDiv from Austin Presbyterian Theological Seminary in Texas. Prior to entering seminary, he worked as a financial advisor in New York City. He lives in Nashville with his wife, Jennifer, and his dog, Chuy. Over the years, he has developed strong feelings about what constitutes chili, and he believes that all meat cooked slowly over a wood fire can be called barbecue.